The
Good
That
Financial
Advisors
Do

Printed in Toronto, Canada. January 2011. The Strategic Coach Inc., 33 Fraser Avenue, Suite 201, Toronto, Ontario, M6K 3J9.

This publication is meant to strengthen your common sense, not to substitute for it. It is also not a substitute for the advice of your doctor, lawyer, accountant, or any of your advisors, personal or professional.

Library and Archives Canada Cataloguing in Publication

Sullivan, Dan, 1944-
     The good that financial advisors do / Dan Sullivan.

ISBN 978-1-897239-18-6

     1. Financial planners. 2. Financial services industry.
I. Title.

HG179.5.S855 2010   332.024   C2010-902831-7

"Being a financial advisor to upwardly mobile individuals in the 21st century is one of the most important roles in our society."

Dan Sullivan

Introduction

The Good That Financial Advisors Do

For almost 40 years, I have been a coach to thousands of financial advisors who come from a variety of mostly English-speaking countries. Not coincidentally, these countries—the United States, Canada, the United Kingdom, South Africa, Singapore, and now India—are among the most prosperous and fastest-growing in the world. In a number of Asian economies, including those of China, Taiwan, Korea, Malaysia, and Vietnam, there has been rapid growth in the number of financial advisors over the past ten years. And numerous other countries in the world will be taking this same path in the coming years of the 21st century.

Prosperity and financial advisors grow together.

There is no question that growing economic prosperity tends to increase the number of financial advisors in a society. And at the same time, there is good evidence to suggest that having many financial advisors in a society also tends to increase the individual prosperity of its citizenry, as well as the prosperity of the whole society. As more individuals use personal financial advisors to plan their financial futures, they achieve higher incomes and savings. They also gain more control over a growing number of long-term practical factors in their personal and professional lives.

These ongoing achievements on the part of hundreds of thousands—and, in some cases, millions—of individuals have a positive collective impact on entire economies. With a rising level of personal financial success for a growing number of people, there are increasing benefits for everyone. A prospering society, in turn, increases the number of individuals who seek out the knowledge and skills of financial advisors.

So it's a chicken-and-egg situation: Which comes first, the prosperity or the advisors? No one can say conclusively, but it is clear that neither development lasts for very long without the other. Those countries with increasing numbers of financial advisors are more likely to grow economically, while those with a declining number of advisors will gradually lose their economic vitality.

Financial advisors benefit not only their own clientele, but society as a whole, in many different ways.

My simple thesis in this little book is that financial advisors are not only good for their individual clientele, but for society as a whole.

To make my case, I have laid out ten reasons why both individuals and societies are better off by having increased numbers of advisors. My hope in writing this is that it will reinforce the financial advisor profession in places where it is already well established, and in many new places as well.

Here is my list of reasons, presented in ten short chapters, followed by four suggested action steps to help advisors move forward into what I believe will be a time of significant new opportunity for those who are tuned in and focused in the right direction.

1.

Long-term, practical financial guidance in a world where change is speeding up and making the future more uncertain.

When I was growing up in northern Ohio in the late 1950s, many of my high school classmates had a goal to work at one of the local auto plants—GM, Chrysler, or Ford. If you could get a job at one of these giant corporations back then, your lifetime financial security was guaranteed.

Large institutions—corporations, unions, and governments—used to provide employees with the financial planning they needed. If you ended up at GM, the corporation would automatically become your financial advisor, career counselor, and retirement planner for the next 40 years of your life. You didn't have to do much thinking or decision-making to have everything taken care of for you.

Throw in the benefits that the union provided, as well as the benefits of the federal and state governments, and your lifetime security and path to success were blueprinted when you were still in your 20s. This was true not only of the automakers, but of many other large organizations, both private and public.

Very little of this kind of corporate or bureaucratic

support and security is still operative in today's world—at least not in the non-government economy. Over the past 30 years, it has become increasingly important for individuals to take personal responsibility for their financial affairs—especially their planning for the future.

"[Financial advisors] become the individual coaches and counselors to replace disappearing corporate and bureaucratic structures that used to provide individuals with security and peace of mind."

This is where the role of personal financial advisors has become so important. Very few people these days have the good fortune of having a guaranteed career. The prediction for a young person entering the workforce today is that he or she may have as many as ten jobs by the age of 65. Employers along the way will only provide current benefits. There will be no long-term guarantees of anything.

It's not just support that individuals no longer receive from their employers—they also no longer receive any guidance on how to look at their personal financial affairs and future.

Knowledgeable and skilled financial advisors, then, provide an invaluable service: They become the individual coaches and counselors to replace disappearing corporate and bureaucratic structures that used to provide individuals with security and peace of mind.

Answer these questions about your own value to your clientele:

1. *As a financial advisor, what are the best examples of current clients to whom you are providing this kind of guidance?*

2. *Who is the financial advisor that you think does the best job at being a great lifetime guide for his or her clientele?*

3. *For you to improve in this role as lifetime financial guide to your clients, what is the biggest improvement you need to make over the next 12 months?*

2.

A solid, evolving lifetime financial game plan that large bureaucracies can no longer provide.

Most large bureaucratic employers today—including many in the financial services industry itself—can no longer guarantee that they will even be in existence ten years from now. And if they can't guarantee their own longevity, it's an even greater certainty that they won't be able to provide much long-term security for those who work for them.

This is an indicator of things to come. The foundations of modern economies are shifting toward a new, more flexible model that provides individuals with more choices in their lives. The flip side of this benefit is that it also requires individuals to take more personal responsibility for their own livelihoods and financial security. All the resources of large organizations must now be focused on their own viability and survival. Few, if any, have the stability or luxury of providing for the long-term welfare of their employees and their families.

"Financial advisors are emerging as the chief providers of plans and strategies for millions."

This new situation is taking hold quickly across modern societies. And whereas previous governments could step in with replacement guarantees, this is less and less possible in the world that is unfolding. Governments themselves are strained to their financial limits and, in the near future, will be forced to start cutting back on guarantees of long-term security even to their own employees.

What this means is that financial advisors are emerging as the chief providers of plans and strategies for millions of individuals who must take greater self-initiative to move upward and forward in their lives, and for many others who simply want to maintain what they've already achieved.

The advisors who are becoming most valuable in response to this enforced self-reliance are those who understand how to work with their clientele to create lifetime financial game plans that can be continually updated and improved.

As an advisor with an opportunity to become more valuable in the marketplace, what are your answers to these questions?

1. *What are your three best examples of providing a successful lifetime game plan for your clientele?*

2. *What are your best opportunities for establishing the same high-quality game plans—or better— with ten more clients within the next 12 months?*

3. *In order to have ten more clients with lifetime game plans, what are the three most important changes you have to make in terms of how you operate as an advisor and as a financial business?*

3.

Providing custom-designed knowledge and wisdom in a world of overwhelming and confusing information.

It is the nature of our world now to make things more complex and confusing. The central cause of this is the explosion of new technologies for creating, storing, and transmitting information from a growing number of sources. This is an exponential—not an incremental—phenomenon.

Knowledge in all areas of expertise no longer grows by adding one thing to what is already known. Knowledge now grows by having everything new multiply everything existing to create even greater new possibilities of multiplying. The age of addition is over; the age of multiplication is now multiplying its impact on us every minute of every day.

To say this is overwhelming and paralyzing for many people is the understatement of the 21st century. But in the midst of all this overwhelm and paralysis is a secret. There is a growing possibility for individuals to achieve increasingly greater clarity, confidence, and capability with the help of a focused financial advisor who knows the following three rules of simplicity:

- You don't need all the knowledge and information in the world—only that which is useful for achieving your individual goals.

- You don't need all the expertise in the world—only knowledgeable and skillful advisors who understand how to keep you informed about changes that are crucial for your individual progress.

- You don't need advisors who know everything about everything—only skilled and responsible individuals who know how, where, and when to find out what you need.

"Knowledge now grows by having everything new multiply everything existing to create even greater new possibilities of multiplying."

In many ways, financial advisors—more than advisors from any other profession or field—are ideally suited to be the most important and useful guides in today's marketplace. They are the only advisors who get to ask their clients about everything related to their past, present, and future. Lawyers don't do this, nor do accountants, doctors, or members of the clergy.

Financial advisors who actively and continually help their clients to evolve their financial plans and achieve their goals are the most important providers of knowledge and strategy.

Answer these questions to see if you fit this central role in the lives of your clientele:

1. *Which three of your clients already look to you as the person they most rely on for crucial knowledge related to their financial and overall futures?*

2. *What are the three most important ways that you are keeping these individuals knowledgeable and informed on an ongoing basis?*

3. *Why and how are you being so useful to these three and maybe not as much to others? Do you want to expand the value you are already providing to these three clients to others? Why or why not?*

4.

A single, personal coordinator of many different kinds of important experts.

Not all experts in today's marketplace are equal in terms of how much value they contribute to the long-term success of their clients or customers. Some experts are useful only on a one-time basis—sometimes just for an event, or sometimes only in a situation that lasts for a few days or even for a few hours.

However, there are experts we need in our lives whose importance and value will extend over an entire lifetime. Medical specialists may be one example, but even most doctors are primarily reactive to our present needs and not proactive in relation to our future aspirations.

Among all experts in today's world, I always put financial advisors at the top of the list of those who have the most enduring importance for the greatest number of consumers in the marketplace.

There are three reasons for my contention:

- The possibility of being able to afford any other kind of expertise during the 21st century depends on having your finances in good order. In order to pay for crucial capabilities in today's world, you need surplus income, which depends upon having guidance, goals, and a game plan.

- The awareness that you need certain kinds of expertise to make improvements in your life depends upon having long-term financial goals and a game plan.

- A financial advisor—more than any other kind of specialist—is more likely to know where much of this crucial expertise can be located and how to secure it.

The best financial advisors I have worked with over the past 30 years were always those who positioned themselves as the active coordinator of a whole network of experts in other fields. For their clients, they were the one expert who knew all the other experts.

Answer these questions to see if you fit the role of being the main provider of crucial knowledge and wisdom to your clientele:

1. *Based on my description of a financial advisor being a single, personal coordinator of other experts, what is your best example of doing this right now for one of your clients?*

2. *How and why did you grow into this role with this particular client?*

3. *A year from now, how could you increase this "coordinator of experts" role in ten more of your most important client relationships?*

5.

Providing a process of shortcuts and time-savers that is impossible for out-siders to understand or implement.

I liken a top financial advisor's abilities to those of a top jazz musician: The world of finances requires continual adaptation and improvisation from a foundation of years of experience and acquired knowledge. Skilled advisors with decades of experience have hundreds of methods and solutions in their heads from their work with thousands of clients.

This is practical wisdom that no one can acquire by going to school or reading books. These advisors know how to cut through the confusion and complications of a new client's situation, and identify decisions and actions that produce immediate progress. From the outside, it may look like magic, but from the perspective of the advisor's experience, it looks like simple logic.

"I liken a top financial advisor's abilities to those of a top jazz musician."

Helping a client to figure out all the complex dimensions of their financial future—and their entire future, on an ongoing basis—is not as simple as reading off of a prepared script. A simple review of what was required to navigate the financial ups and downs in the world since the year 2000 is convincing proof of this statement. New structures, strategies, and solutions have to be created continually in relation to emerging and unpredictable events, situations, and factors.

I find, however, that, even though the best financial advisors are instinctive problem-solvers, they aren't really aware of all the shortcuts and time-savers they have mastered over the course of their successful careers. They don't recognize all the little breakthroughs they have created over the years that, when taken as a whole, represent an extraordinary ability in the eyes of a client.

When I ask some of these top advisors to put their "insider's knowledge and skills" into a unified process and write it down on paper, many important things come to the surface. Once they see their expertise out in the open, they take a big jump in their ability to create new value for their clientele—and to train others on how to do what they do.

Judge your own performance and capabilities in relation to this problem-solving role by answering these three questions:

1. *What are your three biggest time-savers and problem-solving shortcuts that you have mastered since you first became a financial advisor?*

2. *Do you have names for these techniques? If so, what are they? If not, what would be good names for them?*

3. *If you put just these three techniques into a single process you could use with every client, would it improve your performance? How?*

6.

Providing increasing clarity, confidence, and capability that are crucial to your clientele for their individual progress.

Millions of financial advisors around the globe are creating good in the world every day in ways they usually don't see. My goal in this book is to provide an overview of how the work of the best advisors contributes significantly to the progress of individuals and whole societies.

We are living in very different kinds of economies and societies than those that existed even 25 years ago. I contend that personal financial advisors are crucial specialists who enable millions of individuals to adjust to and transform the challenges and opportunities of these new human circumstances.

In this sixth chapter, I will sum up the practical impact and importance of what I have written in the first five chapters. I'll do this by having you answer these five questions:

1. Do you agree that the unpredictable changes in the world are confronting your existing and future clientele with challenges and opportunities that can make you increasingly more valuable to them in your role as a professional financial advisor?

2. Do you agree that in this world of increasing unpredictability, the creation of an evolving, lifetime financial game plan is a crucial tool and process for all individuals who want to take increased personal responsibility for their future success in all areas of their lives?

3. Do you agree that as the amount of information in the world becomes overwhelming, having a skilled financial advisor to provide custom-designed knowledge and strategies becomes necessary for more people to succeed in their 21st-century lives?

4. Do you agree that financial advisors—among all experts that people need in their lives for future success—are best positioned to be the coordinators of many different kinds of specialists?

5. Do you agree that in the course of gaining greater mastery and success as a financial advisor, you have acquired many problem-solving techniques that, if they were organized into a formal process, would

multiply your value in helping your existing and future clientele?

If you answered "yes" to these five questions, then you are also ready, willing, and able to make a quantum leap in your career as a professional financial advisor.

For the rest of your professional life, everything can now be simplified and focused. Your whole purpose in the financial services marketplace is to be the one person who uniquely enables your continually improving clientele to gain greater and greater clarity, confidence, and capability in all areas of their lives.

7.

A professional framework that will be even more valuable 25 years from now.

If you have answered all the questions I've posed so far, then your financial advisor mind is already expanding in new ways. I believe that, if you use this book as a very simple but constant blueprint, you will continually grow as a professional for the rest of your life. Here's how that growth will happen:

First, you will become aware of all the good you already provide to your clientele, and then you will continually find new ways to provide even greater good to them in the future. And you will have no reason to ever stop doing this because the activity of growing in this way will be so personally enjoyable and rewarding.

Your increasing ability to create greater value will also convince you that what you're doing as a financial advisor is one of the most significant roles that anyone can play in the 21st-century marketplace. Not only will this framework of thinking and improvement that you're taking on be more valuable to others, it will be increasingly valuable to you and everyone who works with you and depends upon you.

Over the next 25 years, the whole world is going to continue to change in unpredictable ways. Many large organizations that exist today will not be around after another quarter-century. But all the skills I have laid out in the chapters of this book so far are safe things to count on: You can bet your professional career on these things becoming even more important with each passing year.

"If you use this book as a very simple but constant blueprint, you will continually grow as a professional for the rest of your life."

As the world around you becomes more volatile, your central focus, structure, and process as an advisor will become more solid, successful, and significant to increasing numbers of individuals around you.

To determine how confident you are about what I am suggesting here, answer these three questions:

1. *If you were to use the ideas in this book as the basis for improving yourself as a financial advisor, do you think your confidence and capabilities would be much greater 25 years from now?*

2. *If you continually expand the value of your role as a financial advisor in the ways I am recommending, do you think your value to your clientele will be even greater in 25 years than it is now?*

3. *Do you believe—regardless of how the world, your industry, and your marketplace continually change—that by following this blueprint, you will always be improving and becoming more successful over the next 25 years?*

8.

Taking advantage of superior financial tools and systems that will continually be created to multiply your results.

Do you know what has been the fastest-growing and most profitable industry in the world over the last 25 years?

Some people would immediately say the computer industry, with all of the extraordinary technological breakthroughs that are continually being introduced to hundreds of millions of people. But that answer would be wrong because the computer industry as a whole has actually lost more money than it has made. The total losses of the losers in that industry to date—over the period of the last 50 years—are still greater than the total winnings of the winners.

The right answer to the question is the financial services industry.

The industry you are in is the best in the world at utilizing breakthroughs from the computer industry to continually expand its overall productivity and profitability. I mention this fact simply to emphasize that, as an individual and as a professional, you couldn't be in a better industry over the remaining years of your career.

To be sure, there have been a lot of unpleasant shocks and surprises in financial services over the past quarter-century, and this is just as likely to be true over the next quarter-century. Any industry that attracts the brightest and most ambitious people, makes use of the most powerful technologies, and attracts the most money in the world is likely to be volatile and unpredictable.

At the same time, due to these same factors, you are operating in an industry that is going to continually provide you with a never-ending series of superior financial tools and systems that will make you more valuable as a professional advisor.

"... as an individual and as a professional, you couldn't be in a better industry over the remaining years of your career."

However, to take advantage of these new technologies and techniques, the truth is that you must have the right perspective and be pointed in the right direction. But, chances are, you're someone who is already getting ready for the best possible new capabilities to support your growth and success.

Just to see that this is the case, answer the following three questions:

1. *What are the three technological tools and systems you are already using that have made you a much more productive advisor than you were five years ago?*

2. *Just focusing on these three technological tools and systems you are already using, how can you make even greater use of them—and become even more productive—over the next 12 months?*

3. *Do you believe that—just as you are making use of and will make even greater use of these three technologies—you will also take advantage of new technological breakthroughs over the next 25 years? Why do you believe that?*

9.

Continually learning how the most successful people plan and lead their lives.

Up until now, I have focused on your becoming more valuable to your clientele. Now let's reverse our thinking on these relationships. How much have *you* grown as an individual and as a professional simply because you have been able to develop relationships with your highly successful clients? No doubt you've taken great leaps in terms of your confidence and capability as a result of trying to live up to the expectations of men and women who were more knowledgeable and skillful than you were.

This is actually one of the secret benefits of being a financial advisor that few, if any, other professions enjoy: You get to rub shoulders with more successful people—and learn far more of the secrets of their success—than advisors or experts in any other industry.

In fact, if you were really being truthful with yourself, this is probably one of the things that most attracted you to becoming a financial advisor in the first place. Certainly it was the opportunity to make a good, even great, living. But more than that, it was the even greater opportunity to learn how the most successful people in society got that way—and how they continue to grow and far exceed the normal standards of what most people accomplish over their lifetimes.

"You get to rub shoulders with more successful people—and learn far more of the secrets of their success—than advisors or experts in any other industry."

If you question this, ask yourself how many members of your family and how many of your childhood friends are in as positive a position for growth and success as you are. I'm not saying that you are a superior being because of the advantages and opportunities you presently enjoy. Every person chooses his or her own way in life, and every person chooses what is important and meaningful for them.

There is no comparing the value and meaning of one person's life with another's, but, having said that, you have put yourself in a really good position, given who you were 25 years ago and who you want to be 25 years from now.

Just to prove this to yourself, answer the following three questions:

1. *Which three of your clients—past or present— have you learned the most from about being a successful human being and a successful professional in the marketplace?*

2. *In the future, do you believe you are going to meet and work with other clients who have even greater lessons for you than these three you have listed? Why do you believe that?*

3. *What are the three personal areas where you most want to see improvements over the next three years? What are the three areas as a professional where you want to see the greatest improvement over the next three years? In each case—personal and professional—do you think that there are existing and future clients you can learn from in these areas?*

10.

Being and feeling more and more that you are in the mainstream of human progress.

Most people want to believe that what they're doing is important, not just for themselves, but for everyone else too. In other words, they want to be in the mainstream of human affairs or, better yet, even in the center of human progress.

When you feel that what you're doing is meaningful in this way, you derive enormous confidence from your activities and achievements. You also get a great deal of energy and excitement from the growth of the community and the greater society you're living in, if not from the general progress of humanity as a whole.

I'm writing this to set you up for a great compliment, and here it is: Being a financial advisor to upwardly mobile individuals in the 21st century is one of the most important roles in our society.

Not everyone would agree with this statement, of course, but not everyone's opinion is important here. The opinions and judgments that really count over the course of your lifetime are those of the following people:

- your clients
- members of the support team in your company who help to make you more successful, and into whose lives you help bring more success
- the family members and friends who make your life increasingly meaningful and enjoyable

If all these individuals see that what you're doing is more and more important in their lives, it's a safe bet that you're operating in the mainstream of human progress—and always will be for the rest of your life.

"Being a financial advisor to upwardly mobile individuals in the 21st century is one of the most important roles in our society."

I'm not writing this to give you a big head. This is not about pride, arrogance, or bragging rights. It's simply a matter of recognizing that, for any other kind of progress to occur in the world, people in every situation have to become financially more successful and secure. To do this strategically and systematically over a lifetime, they require skilled financial advisors.

Answer these questions to see if what I'm writing about the long-term importance of your role is true:

1. *What have been your three greatest successes in helping your clients to grow and succeed in their professional and personal lives?*

2. *What have been your three greatest contributions to the growth and success of people who have worked for you?*

3. *In what three ways have you best laid the groundwork for members of your family or your friends to grow and succeed in their lives?*

Moving Forward

1:

The online tool that supports this printed game plan.

All through this book, I've asked you dozens of questions whose answers will represent some profound thinking about your past, present, and future as an advisor. As a coach, I'd be remiss if I didn't give you a way to capitalize on this new wisdom and insight about yourself. So, if you go online to **http://www.strategiccoach.com/goodadvisors**, there is a companion online workbook that you can use to continually develop your thinking about your future as a financial advisor.

As you complete the online workbook, you can go back over your answers to improve them and make them more specific. And you can print copies of your thinking anytime you want.

Accompanying the online workbook is a series of support audios that you can download and listen to at your leisure.

If you'd like to accelerate your growth, progress, and achievement around this book and the accompanying online tools, consider creating a discussion or study group based on this material where each person in the group reads the material, listens to the audios, and then completes the questions. You can do this one chapter at a time over a series of meetings, or focus on two or three chapters at a time.

From almost 40 years of coaching highly successful financial advisors, I've observed that individuals learn most quickly by, one, reading about new strategies and methods; two, thinking about and answering questions that are directly related to their individual self-improvement; and, three, discussing their answers and insights with other individuals who are also motivated to continually improve their careers and their overall lives.

Just to help you organize the possibility of such a study group in your mind, answer these questions:

1. *Who are three financial advisors whose ideas about this book and whose work in the online workbook would be a great benefit to your ongoing thinking and progress?*

2. *How many discussion meetings are you willing*

to commit to over the next 12 months? How many over the next three years? How committed would the other members have to be for you to be interested in being in a group with them?

3. *What are three 12-month benefits from participating in this group that would have to be a real possibility for you before you would consider starting such a project?*

Moving Forward

The regulatory obstacle and its creative bypass.

Over the past 20 years, I have heard one constant complaint from financial advisors, regardless of where they come from around the world: Industry and government regulations are making their work more difficult and their lives less enjoyable.

My take on this is that regulations in any industry are like the weather. You can complain endlessly about them, but eventually, if you're going to lead a more enjoyable and successful life, you have to come up with strategies for protecting yourself from the most unpleasant regulations and regulators.

To be fair to these individuals and their organizations, it has to be said that they are mostly responding to the worst practices and practitioners in the financial services industry—some of whom you know.

As far as large financial services companies go, they are just as burdened by regulations—perhaps much more so—as you are as an individual financial advisor.

If I were in the shoes of an executive or manager responsible for many large financial services organizations today, I would probably be spending much of my time thinking and acting from a defensive position. I would be worrying that out there somewhere at any given time, some of the financial advisors licensed with my organization are doing things that are going to get my company sued, indicted, or attacked in the daily news.

After watching the regulatory wars for the past 36 years, my analysis is that most of the bad things that occur in any financial services company are the result of attempts by companies and advisors to get rewarded without creating anything of lasting value for their clients. The most onerous regulations in place today are the industry's or the government's response to dishonest people coming up with bad concepts and get-rich schemes that never take into account the best interests of consumers in the marketplace.

There is only one way for the financial services industry as a whole, and for advisors within the industry, to create a counterforce to growing regulation: Start thinking about everything and doing everything with the client's long-term best interests as a central focus. I believe that the blueprint I've laid out in this book will help anyone who follows it to avoid regulatory problems in the future, and that it represents a gateway to a new, very positive, and exciting stage in the industry's development.

There are two historical stages of the financial services industry operating in today's world. The first one is an old industrial-age model that is not too different from the way the large auto corporations operated in the mid-20th century in terms of mass production and marketing. Within these large financial bureaucracies, individual clients and customers are seen as "targets" and "statistics." Over the past decade, companies with this outmoded model are continually the target of regulatory agencies.

The second stage of financial services is client-focused. It follows the model and motivations that I have outlined in this book. The new industry is geared to the emerging economies and societies of the 21st century in which individuals want custom-designed planning and services.

The financial companies and advisors who base their development and expansion on client-focused structures will be the ones most immune to regulatory problems.

But if you're not sure of this, I encourage you to work out your thinking about this proposition for yourself by answering these questions:

1. *If you continue to—or begin to—construct the rest of your financial services career based on the observations, strategies, and structures provided in this book, do you think there is any possibility of getting into any kind of regulatory trouble? Why or why not?*

2. *If all advisors in the industry increasingly become more useful and valuable to the long-term success of their clientele as I have outlined here, do you think that the regulatory burdens*

within the industry would increase or decrease over time? Explain your answer.

3. If the entire structure of the financial services industry were based on the principles and strategies of this book, would there be more or less of a need for outside regulation of its affairs? Explain.

3:

The ongoing education and training of the best financial advisors.

All progress in any field is based on continual education and training. Looking at your own development as a financial advisor, if you could start over again, knowing what you know now about the industry and your own future possibilities, how would you design your own educational and training game plan?

I'm guessing one of your most important answers to this question might go like this: "My education and training would be far less about *product* knowledge and far more about *client* knowledge."

The best advisors I have encountered over the past four decades have all known what their products could do, but far more important than their product and technical knowledge, they knew what their clients could do with their lives.

This topic relates to the previous issue regarding regulation. I believe that, to the degree that financial corporations and companies place the main emphasis of their advisor education and training on the maximum marketing and selling of commoditized financial products, they set themselves up for regulatory scrutiny, investigation, prosecutions, and penalties. On the other hand, to the degree that their educational and training programs for advisors emphasize creating maximum value for clientele in the marketplace, they avoid regulatory scrutiny from the very beginning.

"... far more important than their product and technical knowledge, they knew what their clients could do with their lives."

As a matter of prudence then—if only to avoid trouble with regulators in the future—all financial advisor education and training in the 21st century should be client-centered.

This positive, proactive strategy to be client-focused is where the greatest productivity and profitability breakthroughs will lie for financial advisors in the years and decades ahead.

Here are some questions to ask yourself about your own further training and education:

1. *What do you need most for your professional progress: more product and technical knowledge, or much greater understanding of the present issues and challenges, and the future aspirations, of your best clients? Explain your answer.*

2. *What do you appreciate most when you go to company or industry conferences: more product knowledge, or more ideas on how to create value for clients in a changing world? Explain your answer.*

3. *Who do you admire most in the industry: those with the most product knowledge, or those who seem to have great wisdom about what financial services clients want most from their advisors? Give examples and explain.*

Moving Forward

Strategic Coach® and its contribution to the financial services industry.

I've got one goal in everything I do with financial advisors: to multiply their productivity, their profitability, and their enjoyment from being financial advisors. Over the past 20 years, I have created a lifetime educational and training program around this single goal.

Within Strategic Coach®, my associate coaches, my support team, and I have created a continually deepening and expanding system of personal and organizational multipliers that enable entrepreneurially-minded advisors to grow in every part of their lives—for the rest of their lives.

The content of this book is based on literally hundreds of thousands of hours that people in our organization have spent, not only with highly successful financial advisors, but also with thousands of other successful entrepreneurs from over 60 different industries.

You don't have to join the Strategic Coach® Program to benefit from the multiplier concepts and tools we've developed since the 1970s. If you re-read this book on a continual basis, go to the website and fill in the online workbook, and listen to the supporting audios, you will make continual progress. However, if you want to save time and make some significant shortcuts in your professional progress, I can only pass on to you what many of our successful participants have told me:

"I heard about Strategic Coach ten years before I actually signed up for the Program—and I've kicked myself ever since for having waited. If I had signed up when I first had the chance, I would be so far ahead of where I am now."

We have a program—already proven by more than 13,000 successful entrepreneurs—that will quickly begin to multiply the results you're getting in dozens of different parts of your professional and personal life.

Answer these final questions to see if registering for the Strategic Coach Program is the best decision for you right now:

1. *Are you at a point in your professional life where you believe that you have already done the best you can do on your own, and now you need a special custom-designed structure for the next big growth stage in your life as a financial advisor? If so, are you ready to take the next step?*

2. *Who are three financial advisors participating in Strategic Coach whose progress since they signed up has impressed you? What specifically about their progress convinces you that Strategic Coach is the right step for you?*

3. *If you sign up for the Strategic Coach Program, are you ready to make this a normal part of your growth and progress for the rest of your professional life?*

About The Author

Dan Sullivan is the founder and president of The Strategic Coach Inc. and creator of the Strategic Coach® Program, which helps accomplished entrepreneurs reach new heights of success and happiness. He has over 30 years of experience as a strategic planner and coach to entrepreneurial individuals and groups. He is author of over 30 publications, including *The Great Crossover, The 21st Century Agent, Creative Destruction®,* and *How The Best Get Better®,* and co-author of *The Laws of Lifetime Growth* and *The Advisor Century.*